Her Mother's Daughter

By Candi Usher

Table of Contents

Table of Contents 2

Introduction 3

In the Beginning.. 5

The Winds Have Shifted 14

She Don't Want Me No More...................................... 19

Locked Up.. 27

Far, Far Away.. 40

It Won't Heal 48

Digging The Knife Deeper 57

Worst Time In My Life... 64

No More Trying 74

Introduction

I know I'm about to dive into another sensitive subject. Yet, this is mine to touch, and it needs to be done. It's not pretty. It's not glamorous. It's not something everyone wants to talk about. I really don't care how everyone else feels about it. It's something I need to do for me and every other woman who has had issues with her mother, has tried talking them out with her, has tried talking to the therapist, the pastor, the hairdresser, the best friend, and she's tired. She's just plain tired. This book is the scream, the yell, the cry, the words we can't seem to form when we're standing in front of other people, but somehow, we can say them in our heads at 3 am when no one else is around. For some of us, these are the words we'll never be able to say. So, I am giving words to the voices that feel unheard. For the oldest daughter, who feels like she has the weight of the world on her shoulders because she feels like she could never connect with her mother. To the middle daughter who felt like she could never be enough for her mother. To the youngest daughter who always felt like she was reminded of her mistakes, and that was her value to her mother. This book is for the daughters who looked like they were loved by the women who gave them life, but never truly felt loved by them.

In the Beginning

I look back at the pictures of me in the photo albums. I looked like a pretty happy and content baby. I grew up around family and my parents' friends. It looks like they traveled around with me often. I've been told by my birther (I will tell you later why I call her that) that she named me after her favorite singer, Candi Staton (I follow her on Instagram). I've heard that my name was her nickname in the Air Force since her last name was Canady, and they would call her Candi. I don't know if it's true. She said it wasn't, and I've never spoken to any of her Air Force friends to see if it was true or not.

The pictures capture moments where we probably had a much better relationship. Probably when it was appreciated that I couldn't speak my mind as much. I feel like I may have been loved during that time. Is it true? Maybe. Maybe not. My father says it is based on what he saw. Granted, there are times when I wonder. Regardless, it looks like there was some semblance of peace between us.

The pictures also showed me in cute little dresses, bows, and frilly socks with shiny black shoes. She put care into what I wore. It actually seemed to matter to her. Something else that I will go deeper into later. I noticed she took a lot of pictures of me, of me and my dad. She made sure there were plenty of pictures of me and her, too. The clothes and pictures paint a connection of a perfect, or at least a good mother-daughter relationship. Church outfits, family matching clothes, and play outfits were in all the pictures. I was so proud of those pictures growing up, looking at them.

I was told that I had issues with my legs as a baby. Apparently, I was extremely bowlegged. So, my legs needed to be fixed. I had to wear special shoes and all. This delayed my walking. I didn't walk until I was 18 months old, which is much older than most toddlers. It was after we had moved to Georgia, and around when my brother was born.

Oh, the pictures changed when my brother was born. No, I'm not angry about them before anyone gets those thoughts in their heads. He has his own photo album. Well, at least at first he did. They show a lot of him, especially since he was born with jaundice. That meant he had to spend extra time in the hospital, so it took longer for him to come home. According to the parentals, I loved him the moment they brought him home. There's picture evidence that I did. So apparently I did.

Pictures go on to show me and my brother growing up, especially with family. My oldest cousin on my dad's side and the youngest over us were the ones we were the closest to. They were like the big sisters we never had. Our cousin from my dad's side would come visit us, and we would go visit them.

My first memories are at age 5. It was my father's father's funeral. It had snowed in Chicago. It was cold. I remember my grandmother holding me and my cousin close to her. She was crying hard. My dad came to get me so we could leave. My grandma didn't want to let me go. The insane part is I remember details down to the casket. It was white, with gold handles. There are some details from the funeral I won't give just because I don't want to bring pain to other people, and that's just how descriptive those memories are. Why am I telling you this? I need you to understand that my memories go that deep, especially those that hurt me that deep. I remember it all, and in detail.

So, that was all in 1995. In 1996, it snowed for the first time in Georgia in a long time. My brother and I were very excited about the snow. I stayed up most of the night looking out the window, watching the snow fall. When the morning came, I was in a hurry to get dressed and go outside. Don't get me wrong. I couldn't make or throw a snowball for anything in this world. But I wanted to play in the snow, and that was all that mattered. We ate breakfast and got ready to go outside. My dad lambasted my brother and me. My birther helped us for a little bit, but backed out quickly. We lost, but we had plenty of fun.

During that year, I was in kindergarten. The teacher and I did not get along at all. It wasn't that I was a bad student or disobedient. She didn't like that I was on a different level from other students. The teacher's name was Ms Houghbrook. I didn't like that woman at all. She was racist and allowed other kids to pick on me. She paddled me when unnecessary. This woman would get mad when I knew the answers to the questions. My birther was not happy with my treatment in the class, and I can say that was the one point in my life that she actually fought for me. She and Ms Houghbrook butted heads constantly until she was fed up. When the school year ended, so did my attendance at Lakeland Elementary School.

My brother didn't have to go to regular school at that point because of my experience. My parents decided that homeschooling us would be best and more beneficial to us. It gave more control of the curriculum, testing, and hours. My birther had looked into homeschooling groups to ensure that we didn't miss out on having a social life, though a social life didn't matter to me, considering my dad was a minister at the time. I always got to see the friend that I had made at school during VBS in the summers and on Sundays.

The homeschooling let me do things at my own pace, which I loved. The birther still kind of held me back, however. I like to dig my heels in and move. She didn't want me moving too fast. She did push me learning other cultures and how to do things outside the box. Plus, we got to spend more time outside, which I loved the most, as I was a tomboy. When not in schoolwork or outside, my head was stuck in a book, reading, something I got from her. This allowed me to be grade levels ahead when I came to testing for reading and comprehension on the state level.

This was during an age, also from around seven to nine years old, when she dressed me a certain way. Now, I didn't notice it personally, but when I looked at pictures, it shows that certain clothing was chosen that was, ummm, not the best looking. Don't get me wrong. She was nice-looking. Her clothes were on par. She had matching dress sets and nice shoes. Not saying I wasn't dressed decently. Just my clothing was different. My birther also had me and my brother's clothes made, which she didn't have to considering my dad worked several jobs. Food and clothing were affordable. But still...

I also realized during this time that my brother and I had gone through many fights. Not trying to hurt each other, but we did a lot of hitting and wrestling. Some things happened that weren't the best between us. At times, we would be spanked for doing stupid stuff like jumping off the roof or something else that was really dumb. If I had an attitude, I would write how I felt about how my birther treated me. There were times when I felt the punishment didn't fit the crime. When I hid the tables that I wrote in, somehow they magically found their way to my birther, and she was reading my words. There was absolutely no privacy. I would write how much I hated her. No, I didn't truly hate her, but I didn't like her at all. I felt very disconnected from her. At points, I would get a spanking where my brother wouldn't, or he would get off punishment sooner than me. We would be placed on punishment for a certain number of hours at a time. You can guess which one of us served the most hours.

    At this age, I had also given my life to Christ. Yes, I had my usual kid actions. Yet, I loved God. I loved talking about Him to everyone. Being a preacher's kid and Pastor's grandkid was everything to me. It wasn't something I needed to brag on, yet it was what I was proud of. Whenever I had the chance, I would tell people about Jesus. I had I fire for God. For me, going to church was fun, but the ride to and from church was more fun. We used to play a game called Find the Scripture. You not only had to find the scripture first, but read it too. I had it down to a too. There were points where I was forced to find the scriptures because I had them memorized. I realize now that those were again sore points for my birther. I didn't study. It was like the Word clicked for me. I could read it, and I understood. I could easily speak to people, no matter what age, about Christ. Sometimes it felt like I had no fear. It would just well up and come out. I never minded serving God. I later found out that this was a prophecy spoken over my life before I was even born.

Somewhere during this time, my birther decided she wanted me to be ladylike. So, she decided it was a good idea to put me through etiquette. I hated every moment of it. I had to learn how to set a table and sit properly. I had to walk around with a book balanced on my head so my back would be straight, and I walked properly. I learned to curtsy and properly do a handshake. These are things still stuck in my head to this day.

During one of the summers, we went to a pool party at a church member's house. At one point, my brother had ended up in the wrong end of the pool, and had to be rescued. My birther ran to him, hugging him and wrapping him in a towel, concerned about him almost drowning. Sometime later, I still don't even remember how,

I ended up in the deep end of the same pool, too. I remember calling for my dad. He grabbed my arm and pulled me to the top. I didn't even feel like I was drowning, even though I was at the bottom of the pool when he reached me. My dad wrapped me in a towel and made sure I was ok.

The Winds Have Shifted

Now we move into a challenging portion of my life. My birther decided that she wanted to go to school to be a teacher like my father was. That meant my brother and I had to go to public school. I didn't want to go because I liked being homeschooled. My freedom and control were going to be gone. I had no choice.

I started seventh grade at J. L Newbern with odd stares. I was automatically known as Mr. Usher's daughter. Most of the students knew my dad because he had been their teacher the year before. Most of the guys knew him because he had coached the football team. I didn't have my own identity.

My clothes, shoes, and hair were not like any of the other girls. I didn't act like any of them. I certainly didn't speak like any of the kids in class. I was told I speak proper and uppity. I felt how I spoke was normal. Yet that, my clothes, and my skin tone became the reasons for a girl and her friends to start picking on me. I was called blackie, tarbaby, darkie, beanpole, four eyes, old lady, bougie, and so many other names. It was like knives were being stuck in me daily. It made me hate going to school. When I told my birther what was happening and how I felt, her answer was to pray for them and ignore them. That was some of the greatest pain I felt from her. The words came from a woman who grew up in segregation and went through desegregation. She knew what being called outside of your name was. She was born and raised in the South. Her parents were born and raised in the South. There was no sympathy or empathy from her. My birther expected me to suck it up and deal with it. Yet, when my brother suffered from bullying at S.L. Mason, guess who was to his rescue? Exactly.

  I suffered in silence. I should have said something to my dad, but fear of retaliation toward him, more than anything, kept me silent. I knew how vicious kids could be based on how vicious they had been to me. The words sent me down a spiral that stayed mainly between me and God. I never told anyone what was happening. I smiled on the outside, dying on the inside. Thoughts on suicide ran through my mind often. My attitude changed a lot. Hormonal changes didn't help much either. I was not happy much at all. I could tell that my birther was different. I just didn't know why she was so different.

Another thing I noticed was how much she and my dad argued. I had never seen them have so many disagreements in my life. It felt like every other day; they had an issue. Something was always going wrong. The family as a whole was spending less and less time together. My birther was spending less and less time with us as she was spending more and more time at school. Those were some of the last summer trips we took out of town. Things were falling apart, and there was nothing that could put them back together.

Vacation Bible School (VBS) came around again during those summers, too, and my torture began. There was this one kid who liked me and picked on me every chance he got. My birther never explained that when middle school-aged boys liked middle school-aged girls, they picked on them every chance they got. This boy teased me whenever he could. He seemed to be at every Vacation Bible School event at every church in our little city. I couldn't escape him, no matter how bad I tried. His dad was a minister too, and our parents knew each other. It was brutal. I couldn't talk to my birther. The conversation I would watch the girls on TV have with their mothers, I knew I couldn't have with my birther.

This was the age for "the talk." You know—the sex education conversation. I now wish it had been anyone else but my birther that I would have had that conversation with. Why? When I had "the talk" with my sons, I told them the truth about what it's like for girls because I need them to understand the pain they will put her through if it's her first time. My birther did not tell me the full truth. Her end of the conversation? A man and a woman shouldn't have sex until marriage. Sex before marriage is wrong. That's about it. There was nothing in depth. Nothing that would explain the first time, say why the first time should be waited on, nothing about a relationship being important from a wife's perspective, that a daughter needed to know.

I've always been a bit of a tomboy. As I sit here typing this, I realize that this is the juncture in my life where I realize I changed to try to get her attention for the first time. I used to despise skirts and dresses heavily. I never felt very comfortable in them. Yet for her, I was willing to put them on for a while. Huge mistake. I may as well have made myself even more invisible.

I was into the same sports that she liked. I loved basketball and baseball. I played softball after having to transition from T-ball because girls weren't allowed to play T-ball after a certain age. I didn't like softball as much because the attitudes of the girls clashed a lot. You talked about a bunch of hormones all at one time. Add on issues with the birther, and let's just say I was happier being on the field than being at home.

She Don't Want Me No More

Now we enter my teenage years. I started high school in 1998 at the great Valdosta High School. My father was the pastor at Irvin Hill Baptist Church. Why do I bring these things up? Because these places are going to have some meaning.

Freshman year is awkward for everyone. You're making adjustments. You've kind of figured out who you are since the beginning of that school year and the end of the eighth-grade year. Some of your friends have followed you over. You have some new people to meet. Valdosta High had a new ninth-grade wing that was separate from the main high school, so we had most of our classes over there. Granted, you did have some of your holdbacks integrated.

That same year, there was an entire personality shift in my birther. She began coming home late at night. The arguments between her and my father weren't violent, but she would slam doors. There were times she would get in the car and just leave for no reason I could understand. She and I bumped heads harder, also. Everything I did was wrong, no matter how right I did it. She was making weird noises in church while my father was preaching. Like random noises on purpose. All attention had to be on her.

Punishments with her also became severe. She would put my brother and me outside if we did something wrong: no shoes or anything on our feet. There were plenty of cold nights when my father pulled up to the house at ten or eleven at night, and I was on the front porch shivering where I had gotten into a disagreement with my birther and she had put me outside. I may have been out there for almost 30 minutes by the time he pulled up. He was not happy about it at all. Those moments also affected my grades. One night, she woke me up for failing a quiz. My birther slapped me across the face. I was in shock because she had never hit me like that before. About an hour later, she came in and told me to hit her back. I couldn't even do it. The tears that streamed down my face were so heavy. At that moment, I felt she was gone. I didn't even know who she was.

Things eventually got so bad that my father felt my birther needed treatment. At some point while my brother and I were in school, my birther was placed in a psychiatric ward in

Thomasville, GA. It was kind of rough knowing she was there. I knew she was sick, but a teenage brain couldn't comprehend why she was that sick, and how she could be that sick. We would visit her several times a week so she could know that we still loved her, and she could see how we were doing.

One of those trips was the trip that made me never want to go back ever again. That day crushed my entire soul. We were sitting there talking to my birther, and suddenly she told us that she didn't have to come back home. She told my brother and me she didn't want us anymore, but she never looked at my brother. She looked right at me. In that moment, I never felt more unwanted in my life. That was the moment that began the domino effect for seeking validation for me. As a child, words have always held meaning. They were always my validation, my encouragement, my everything. It only took four to rip my entire world apart, my self-esteem, and begin my spiral into self-doubt and people pleasing. I don't even think it mattered to her.

I was like a shell of a person after that. I felt like days just blended together. Eventually, she came home, and I did everything I could again to change myself to please her. She didn't want me, but I was bent upon making her want me. I didn't know how to just give up and leave it alone. Her words affected my school life, however. I distanced myself from many people I hung around with. I became part of the Emo kids. It just felt better being around them. They understood where I was in life at that point, better, I guess. Maybe I was in a dark place and just didn't realize it. I know that when I reached out, they were there. Most of the people I would usually hang around, I didn't feel would understand what I was going through, or I felt didn't notice the issues.

    I knew the church wasn't paying much attention. That hurt more than anything to me at the time. Here my family was going through something that painful, and we were being ignored by the people who should see us the most. No one from any church spoke to me at any point about what was going on and checked on me or my brother that I knew of. My faith in God began to wane. I seriously felt withdrawn and distant from Him. Church was a place to be. Yet, that's all it was. It was a function. It wasn't the joy it used to be. Reading the Bible and growing with God wasn't what it used to be anymore.

Time continued to pass, and the pain continued to grow. My birther went to the psych ward again. When she came home again, it was hard trying to live with her. It was like having a ghost in the house. Sometimes I felt like I was walking on eggshells. Other times, I felt like I wanted to explode. A part of me needed to please her, and another part needed to be as far away from her as possible.

When I hit my junior year of high school, I had become a loner at school because of everything happening. I just didn't want to be attached to anyone any more than necessary. That left me open for the wrong person to get attached to me. His cousin started coming around me first. Then he started coming around me, wanting to date me. He gave me the words of validation I wanted to hear from my birther. What I didn't realize was that I was allowing her into my life in a different form. While we were dating, he offered to allow me to move in with him and his family so I could get away from the issues I was having with my birther. I took it offer because I knew if I stayed home any longer, things were going to explode. It was going to be me or her, and the violence was not going to end well. I had begun having blackout moments, which were dangerous and unhealthy.

During the time this person was invading my life, my grandfather passed. It was rough on my birther's side of the family. My father was a support to her, even though the two of them had been having so many issues. That side kept trying to tell me I needed to go home. I was trying to explain to them how my birther had been treating me and why I didn't want to go home. Some of them were the same ones I had reached out to and asked to move in with before I left home because of the issues. I didn't understand wanting me to go back to that house, knowing what the situation was. I believed they didn't care, and I felt as thrown away by them as their sister/aunt/daughter/niece made me feel and treated me.

The leech in my life made it like a living nightmare. Yet, I would rather be with him than be with my birther. Both of them used words to destroy me in their own way. I know to most people it doesn't make sense that I would rather be with someone who was treating me worse than my birther was, but in my teenage mind, the grasp was different. With him, I could at least fight back. I could defend myself. I felt defenseless against my birther. Though I wanted to strike back against her, respect for her as my parent would not allow me to go that far.

The relationship with the leech got worse and worse as time went on. He had already homed in on the verbal abuse that had started with my birther. He then moved to using the fact that I had isolated myself at school. I was getting to the point where I wanted to isolate myself from him, and he wasn't going to allow the control he had over me to slip. The leech had my brother jumped by some boys in the lunchroom when we were being let in for class one morning. He gave me an ultimatum. Stay with him, or my brother will continue getting beaten up. I chose to stay. In the end, I ended up with more than just the verbal, mental, and emotional abuse. Like with my birther, there was physical abuse also. He made sure they were hidden so no one could see them.

Everything for me was placed behind a smile. I smiled so everyone would think things were okay at home. A smile hid the pain of the abusive relationship with my birther and my then-boyfriend, although people saw and knew things weren't okay. I didn't know whom I could trust. One day, it all became too much.

Locked Up

Now we head into the journey of my adulthood. Eighteen years old and finally finished school. I attempted suicide at one point. With everything happening with my birther, my boyfriend treating me like trash, cheating, and having us homeless, then his stepfather attempting to rape me and his feeble attempt to defend me, I no longer wanted to live. I felt the world would be better off without me. I no longer wanted to live. I had given up. I had thrown myself away. I had cut my wrists, ready to die. But God said it wasn't my time. My boyfriend found me and covered the wound on my left wrist. I had no choice that day but to live.

After all of that, the leech turns around and goes to jail. He has me leave the house we were staying in so his still married and pregnant girlfriend could have somewhere to stay with her children. I was livid. Yet, I left because I felt bad for the kids. A few days later, I didn't feel good, so I went to get tested for pregnancy. I was pregnant. It was the worst time to find out I was having a baby, especially with him. Yet, I was happy that I was getting the chance to be a better mother than the one I had been.

I did tell my birther I was expecting. Then suddenly, she shows up all lovey-dovey and caring. She made sure I had food. She would pick me up and take me back to the house. I started receiving the attention I craved growing up. Yet, it felt off. It wasn't genuine. My birther was bending over backwards for the baby. Showing up for doctor's appointments. She would drive me where I wanted to go when she was in town. I thought she was trying to rebuild our relationship. Blame me for being so naïve.

My dad was disappointed in me, and rightfully so. He did not care for the leech. They did not like each other. The leech tried to bend over backward to please my father. My father knew he had my brother jumped. He thought my dad didn't know anything about his cheating and how he treated me. Yet he put up with him for my sake and the sake of our child. My then-boyfriend turned husband (oh, he married me) temporarily changed his face to look good in front of everyone.

My birther was present at the birth of my son. I cussed and fussed a storm. She didn't like my language, and I honestly didn't care. Where was the leech, aka husband? With his friend and another woman. How do I know? He came in right when I was pushing my son out, smelling like another woman, his friend walking in right beside him. They were laughing and smiling like I wasn't in pain and like nothing was happening. My birther was no help in the situation. My son came into this world with my love, and the vow that I would never be like my birther. She loved all over him like he was the greatest thing ever to happen, but my heart knew better. It felt like there was a hole in my soul.

    My birther ended up taking me home since the leech had to work when it was time to leave the hospital. She didn't want to be in the hospital room at the same time as my father for whatever reason at that time. I didn't know that the birther had filed for divorce at that point. There was a lot of tension. I hoped that maybe my son could possibly make her talk to my father, but that was not going to happen. I was happy to finally go home and be in my own space again. A few days later, my birther offered to do newborn pictures for my son. She seemed to be happy to be a grandma at that point. The problem with that? She also thought that meant she could tell me what to do when it came to my son. That soon became a really big problem.

We went to take the pictures, and it seemed that everything was going well. Then things started to take a turn for the worse. This was in 2003, when Walmart used to have a photography place. The birther started off with the outfit. Then there was an issue with the shoes. Once we finally got the pictures taken, we were finally able to get out of there, only for her to somehow lose her purse. The day became a complete nightmare. I was tired and I just wanted to sleep. I knew that the leech wasn't going to be around because his girlfriend was more important at the time. My emotions were high.

Eventually, we had to move out of the place we were staying in because even though the leech had a job, somehow the money wasn't being put back into the house. My father came with his truck to help us move. Right after he pulled up, the leech's girlfriend pulled up. She was not happy with the leech. I don't know how, but somebody gave somebody else an STD. Thank God that I was not sexually active with him at that time. Oh, and did I mention that the house that he was moving us into was hers? Yeah. She was moving out, and he was moving us in. My life was mad messy, and it was getting messier. By the way, the woman was leech's stepdad's supposed niece on top of that and had introduced them. What person connected their married stepson intentionally to their niece? If you hate, just say so. Please and thank you.

    I thought moving would bring peace. I was more than wrong. It was just me, my son, and leech for a little while, with his brother and sister coming to stay with us from time to time. Then magically, out of the blue, a random cousin shows up. I've been with this person for two years, and that "cousin" never existed. Now, not only does she exist, but she exists in my house. Adding salt to the wound is that my father and the birther were divorced. The birther decided she wanted to walk away from the very person who would walk the world and back to help her. So, my dad and brother lived right across the street from me. Which meant all my pain was seen by them. Embarrassed didn't begin to describe what I felt.

    There was one night when the leech asked me to take his sister home after she had spent the night at our house. I didn't have a problem with it. My son was asleep, and since it was late enough at night, there weren't many people on the road. The trip wouldn't take too long. I dropped his sister off and came back to the house. Something inside said not to make too much noise when I got back to the house. I get to my room to find the leech having sex with his "cousin," my son in his basinet, screaming. They acted like they didn't even hear him. Obviously, this was not their first time, and apparently they felt they thought I would take longer than what I took. Violence doesn't begin to describe what I thought and felt.

When I told my birther what happened, she told me that's what I deserved for choosing to be with him. I'm hurting from a blow like that, and that's what you say? I felt like she had punched me in my chest. At the same time, I felt like I had to suck it up and deal with it. I had nowhere to go. I couldn't stay with my dad at the time. I wasn't going to stay with my birther. None of my other family members had somewhere for me and my son. The leech had made it very clear that if I left him, he would take my son, and I would never see him again.

See, the relationship if you could call it that, had gotten physically abusive. We were physically fighting at times. He would never hit me where it would show, however. Always in places that didn't bruise much, but left enough pain. Fighting with my brother pushed me to always fight back. I didn't know how to back down at any point. Pour on him regularly messing with old girl, and basically having his cake and eating it too, because that's exactly what it had become. It was dangerous to be in that house, and even more dangerous to be with him.

The two of them had more things going on behind my back than I knew. They would leave and go places and not come back until late at night or until the next morning. There were times when the leech would get me to ask my dad to borrow his car. At one point, we got pulled over in my dad's car, the police office coming to my side specifically (the passenger side). The officer had me open my door and step out of the car. I went to the back and grabbed my son. For whatever odd reason, the officer reached straight into my door. What did he pull out? A dime of bag of weed that I had no idea was in there. Everyone looked at me like I was going to take responsibility for it. They had all lost their mind. Leech ended up in jail that night. I don't know how he got out, but he did. It didn't last long. A few weeks later, he was right back in for violating probation. When he went in, I made sure I put the girl out not too long after. I had enough to deal with.

    I was right about enough to deal with because the birther started showing back up again. She figured it was a good idea to come around again since she didn't have to look at the leech as much anymore. My friend from church moved in with me so I wouldn't be in the house by myself. Her boyfriend moved in, too, to help make sure we were safe. With my friend and her boyfriend being there, I had a babysitter when I had a bacterial meningitis scare and had to be rushed to the hospital. My birther didn't like them being there at all. This woman showed up at my house, threatening to call child protective services on me. The thing is, she couldn't even give me a valid reason. It got to the point where I had to call the police before she would leave. Apparently, she went to her mother's house from there or whatever because I received a call from her fussing at me, reminding me that my birther had mental issues. I should have called her or another "family member" to handle the issue, and not the police. Apparently, the birther was having another mental breakdown, and she needed "extra love." Basically, they were telling me to cater to her. I caved because, yet again, I wanted to please the birther and her mother. There were consequences for those actions.

My dad had moved on with his life and began dating. My brother had moved into his place and was moving toward getting married. It felt strange because all I knew was him and my birther all my life. My biggest fear was that when my dad remarried, his new wife wouldn't want me. One thing about words is that they can bury deep into your soul like seeds and take root deeper than weeds. My fear was going to show eventually.

I ended up losing my place because my friend ended up moving out, and funds were just not there. I had to move to low-income housing for a little while so I could get back on my feet. During my time with the leech, I lost a lot of contact with my friends, especially my sisters, who were my bestie and the other was my cousin. I reconnected with both of them, which I needed in my life so much. I also moved on and began dating. Yes, it was messed up, considering I was still married on paper. At that time, I didn't care if the man knew what I was doing since he was behind bars, and he didn't care how he treated me when he was in my face. That was not the best decision at the time.

I received a phone call one day asking me to come into the sheriff's office for some questioning about the leech. I didn't have any problem with it, considering I had nothing to hide, and I didn't participate in anything that the leech and the girl who had stayed with us did. I took my son with me, thinking it wouldn't take too long. The detective asked me questions about certain nights when the leech and the girl left and if I was with them. He claimed that I was supposedly identified as a person with the leech in two armed robberies. The problem with that is that both of those nights, I had an alibi. The leech purchased the girl two outfits that were identical to mine, and there were several times when her hair was done exactly like mine was. The beautiful thing was that my father and God were looking out for me. When he noticed the girl dressing like me or intentionally doing her hair like me, he would tell me he didn't like my hair or outfit. I would change both before leaving home. People would never see us in public with the same thing on or with our hair the same. The leech still made a statement against me, claiming I helped him with two of the armed robberies. I found out in the process that he had done six in all. The girl had been accused of doing the other four with him. I tried to call knew my birther couldn't take my son because of her mental issues. The leech's family couldn't come near my son because they had had their own issues with child protective services. My dad wasn't able to take my son because of scheduling, and social services refused to allow my best friend, his godmother, to even take him. So, my son was basically ripped from my arms by social services. Both of us were broken and crying, forced to go away from each other in two different directions.

    Now for the crazy part. I ended up in a cell with the girl. Not the same room, but the same cell. She thought I wanted to attack her. She wasn't worth the time or attention. I had the custody of my son and fighting my charges to worry about. My focus was on my court dates and dealing with the leech. He was sending letters through his mother, talking about what he claimed he could do for me. I found out he accused me of the two armed robberies because he found out I was dating, and he didn't want someone else around "his son" (he didn't care about my son at all), and I had been messy and dedicated the song "Let It Burn" by Usher to him over the radio a few weeks before. So, he had decided he was going to get his payback, even though I had nothing to do with any of it.

I was also receiving letters from the birther. At the time, she was staying with her mother. She, her birther, and my dad had been attending court dates to check on progress for attempting to get at least temporary custody of my son until we could get my charges fixed. The judge didn't want to allow anyone to take him. The judge was already biased due to the fact that he had dealt with the leech when he was growing up. He had been in and out of his courtroom, and he thought my son would end up the same way. I had already made up in my mind that the sins of the leech were not going to be that of my son. I had an uphill battle to fight.

I had visitations on Saturdays, which helped me push through the weeks. There were times I wanted to give up so bad. The leech was trying to get me to plead guilty to charges that I wasn't even guilty of, claiming he had people who would say they saw me. The birther was telling me I should never have gotten involved with him and that it was my own fault that I was in the mess I was in. My dad was the only one fighting for me. He had found a lawyer for me who took my case, and she did her thing. She confirmed both of my alibis, and my charges were dropped. I spent ninety days in jail. I walked away Scott-free. That was nobody but God. The thing was, while I was in there was a guard I used to talk to. I said things to her out of fear about my dad moving on in his life, and how I was unsure about the woman he was considering marrying. I did not trust her at all. I hadn't met her or spent time with her like my brother had. In my mind, there was a loyalty I still needed to show to my birther, regardless. My stupidity would come back to bite me hard.

Far, Far Away

I was released to start my life all over again from scratch. I moved in with my birther's birther for about two weeks. The time was short because it was not working for either of us. She wanted to basically place me under major restriction. It was already enough that my son was in a city hours away, so visitation was only at times. My brother had gotten me a job at his McDonald's so I could get a place and get back custody of my son. I found out that God opened the door for me to get out right on time because the family who was fostering my son was trying to adopt him. Now I want it noted that during this time, my birther did not ask to come to any of the visitations. She didn't ask if they could be moved for her, or even if she could call and talk to my son during the visits. I was ready for something different.

Time went past, and I was finally able to get custody of my son back. Not long after, though, I lost the new place I had gotten, making stupid decisions. My son and I were living in a homeless shelter. My life was in shambles. I had been going back to church and figuring out what I needed to do to get my life back together. I wanted out of Valdosta, sooner rather than later. My spiritual mom was picking me up from the shelter and taking me back and forth to service at one of the churches I grew up in. I felt drawn to follow in the family footsteps (dad's side) and go into the military. The hardest part of that would be having someone to keep my son so I could go to boot camp. The leech's stepfather's sister worked at the shelter and offered to keep my son if I decided to join. My mind was made up to leave.

Eventually, I began to talk to my soon-to-be stepmom. The thing was, I wasn't the nicest to her. I standoffish. She was kind enough to do my hair for me. I can say that I never gave her the chance she should have had to begin with. I was distant. I was still trying to show my birther that she could still want me. I was still worthy of her love. I was hurting myself more than I realized.

I made my way to the Air Force office, as that was the branch I had decided to do. I wanted to follow directly in the footsteps that were in front of me. The thing was, they wouldn't take me. I was considered a single parent since the leech and I were still married, and he was in prison. Oh yeah. He pleaded guilty to all six of his charges and received thirteen years in prison. We still hadn't divorced yet because I didn't have the money to file. So, I had to find another branch to join. I ruled out the Army and Marines, so I headed to the Navy office. They signed me up and sent me for my ASVAB. I did well on it, even though I was older than almost the entire class I took it with. I went to MEPS in Jacksonville, FL, to do my medical exam and do my swearing-in. Unfortunately, a lump was found in my left breast, which meant surgical removal and testing. The problem was finding a way to cover the surgery because Medicaid wouldn't take care of it. I began praying.

Later that summer on Juneteenth, my dad and mom (not talking about my birther) married. It was a nice wedding, and we had an amazing time. My brother and I tore up the dance floor. I knew this was going to be the last time I was with a lot of these people. I wanted to hold on to as many of those moments as possible. We took many pictures and hung out.

A few weeks later, I went to the hospital for surgical removal of the lump in my breast. I managed to get a grant through the shelter. I also had to lean on the birther as far as staying with her after surgery, because someone had to keep an eye on me afterward. She had her apartment, and it meant I didn't have to trust someone else to watch my son, even though I didn't want to trust her. I didn't do well with anesthesia, something she so politely passed to me. That was a long twenty-four hours, as she was like her birther and wanted things her way. I was never happier to go back to the shelter.

    Several weeks later, the results were in that the lump was a fibroid. I checked out of the shelter, spent the last night with my son where he would be staying until I was settled at my first duty station, and cried myself to sleep. My heart was heavy as I left Valdosta for the last time. I say the last time because the week before, I had promised my dad that when I left, I would not be moving back. Granted, like I said before, I wanted to leave, but this was actually happening. We arrived at MEPS, completed processing, then ate and rested for the night. We got up the next morning and boarded the flight headed to the Great Lakes, Michigan. I arrived to begin the journey of my life. The phoenix had burned herself in Valdosta and was being reborn from ash in Great Lakes.

That was the most insane seven weeks of my life. The days went by quickly because there was so much to learn in a short amount of time. It was September when I arrived. The RDCs were adamant about getting us out before Thanksgiving, so they were going to push us as hard as possible. The thing was, I couldn't swim. So, in the process, while learning to march, exercising, learning all the knots, ship basics, Navy history, and all the other necessities, plus having my wisdom teeth removed and going through recovery, I had to learn how to swim. As you can see, I made it. What kept me going was being able to make weekly phone calls and letters from home. The birther made a point to send the letters. She had also taken my son to take another set of pictures. I made a point to push so I could give him better. It was rough in boot camp, not because of the pressure of the RDCs, but because of the dumb young girls who wouldn't listen. I detest not following instructions. If you're told to shut up and get in line, do what you're told. We had in trouble so many times because the young heads wouldn't listen. When I tell you I was ready to fight so many times, it wasn't funny. My dad always told me I was a leader, not a follower. I just knew that I had gotten fed up. One of the RDCs had given us the option that if we were tired, we could quit. I got up and left. It wasn't because I was tired, but it was because I was at the point that I wanted to fight, and it wasn't going to end well in that barracks room. He and the female RDC chased me down and talked to me. They could both see my frustration. They also knew about my son and my goals. Once I was calm, I was allowed to vent, and vent I did. I was glad when boot camp was over after boot camp was a different story.

Graduation day came in with snow that melted by the time the ceremony was over. My dad is from Chicago, which isn't but a few hours from Great Lakes. The arrangement was to spend the night at my aunt's (my dad's sister) house after graduation, because I was going to Valdosta for Thanksgiving and my brother's wedding. Plus, I wanted to see my son and make sure he was doing ok. The time in Chicago also allowed me to see my grandmother, whom I hadn't seen in years, and my little cousins. I got on the train and got to Chicago, having to wait for several hours until I was able to meet with my aunt. I wish the visit had been better. It wasn't the visit I thought it would be. It was more about my dad and him remarrying, than me being about to talk about dealing with the birther. Conversation about my son? He didn't matter. Which was crazy considering he's the oldest great-nephew and great-grandchild. Sad part? My dad's mother met my son once in his entire life. He wasn't even two. She met none of my other children. This same grandmother picked me up from my aunt's house and paraded me around, showing off the granddaughter that she was so proud went into the Navy. As I write this, I realize that I've been thrown away by a number of women in my life, and that I showed them all a level of dedication they didn't deserve.

    The next day, I left Chicago for Valdosta, glad to see my son and family. I was in my Navy dress blues for my brother's wedding. I felt uncomfortable at his wedding. The trip just didn't feel normal in and of itself. I still wasn't responding to Mom like I should have been. I was bending over backwards for the birther again. She and her birther were so proud to tell everyone that I was in the Navy. Yet, they still didn't hesitate to remind me about being married to the leech either. I couldn't wait until I had the paperwork together so I could get rid of him from my life.

Next stop was Meridian, Mississippi, for A school. This was where I learned my job for the Navy. I had chosen to be a Yeoman, which was basically a secretary, a job I had been doing since I was thirteen. My dad gave me the job in his accounting business when I came of age. It gave me great training and came in handy when I came into my own. From there, I got my orders to my first duty station in California. I was moving far, far away.

It Won't Heal

California was so beautiful. I was so happy to be there. Yet, in all my intelligence, instead of going there first, checking it out, getting things in order, then bringing my son, I grabbed him and ran to Cali. Yes, I'm aware that it was dumb and stupid. I was running from any and everything at the time. I was running from every decision, choice, situation, conversation, person I needed to face, person I hurt, thing I said, everything. As far as I was concerned, God had answered the prayer, and the rest could be played by ear.

What I forgot was everyone else I had involved in my selfishness. I was dating a guy who moved out with me to help with my son. First, that wasn't fair to him because I was still married. The thing was, he didn't know that. To me, it didn't matter because it was only on paper. It still wasn't right, however. Also, I put him in the predicament of not being able to find a job to help, no more than taking care of my son when he wanted to contribute to the house. When you play with God, you pay a price. I played in God's face, and God popped me hard for it. The guy ended up finding out about me hiding my marriage from him, he left, and I had to find another way to take care of my son. Granted, another door did thankfully open.

I finally filed for my divorce. I sent the birther the paperwork, had her file, and got the court date. I wanted to move on with my life freely. I was done having the leech's last name cuffed to me. I had already cut off communication with him. When conviction eats you, it hits hard. When God has chosen you for something, things in life hit you differently.

While waiting on that process, I found my tribe at my command. I connected with the most amazing woman in the world. I found my new sisters. They had my back through it all. When I had duty, they helped with babysitting. I also found a babysitter for when we were at work. The only issue was when I had to serve in the galley. The galley is like the lunchroom. The thing about serving in the galley is you have to be there from 4 a.m. to 12 p.m. It's hard to find a babysitter that early in the morning. I knew I would have to, unfortunately, take my son back home again. That meant we would have to separate again. The command wanted me to move into the barracks so it would be easier for me. I wanted my son with me, but there was no choice.

When I went home for my divorce that October, I ended up having to take my son back to the same house that I had removed him from. I didn't like it, but there wasn't much of a choice. I felt like I was pulling my heart out of my chest all over again. I was starting to wonder if I had made the right decision in going into the Navy. My cousin had to remind me that the sacrifice I was making right then was going to pave a permanent road that would mean my son would never have to come back to that city. I took that and made that my anchor and focus.

The most beautiful part of the trip was getting the divorce decree. Those papers that said that not only was I free from leech, but that I had my original name back. I thought about changing my son's name, but that came with a lot of hassle. Plus, it wouldn't help if I wanted child support later. Finally, things were starting to get better. At least, that's what I thought.

I went back to Cali, going on with life. I checked on my son, making sure money went home to take care of him. Eventually, I moved him from the aunt's house to his godmother's/my bestie's house. I had more trust since I found out the leech's stepfather's sister was being abusive toward my son. She was allowing her children to take my son's food that my money was paying for, and dressing him in old clothes when I was purchasing him new ones. The thing is that the birther wasn't telling me about it, even though she was aware of it. Who let her off the hook, though, because her case was pleaded by lapse of mental illness? Her birther kept fighting the battle for her, and I kept caving in. I'm sure by now you have a lot of thoughts of me. I'll address as many as possible at the end of the book.

My bestie and my dad worked together to do the best for my son. He was placed in daycare that was great for him and boosted his childcare. He started with my grandma (Mom's mama), then moved to my bestie's aunt. They both encouraged his intelligence and growth. The birther and my brother would get him on the weekends and take him to church. Here's the thing about that. There were a few times when they got into car accidents. When did I find out? Much later on. After my bestie found out much later on. This was information we needed to know as soon as it happened, and everyone was either checked and okayed or sent to the hospital. I needed to know if the Red Cross needed to be notified and have me on standby to go home. I needed the status of my son. To know that I was placing the safety of my child in their hands, and them not letting me know what was happening, was building a level of distrust that I didn't like at all.

    Soon, the time in Cali was coming to an end. My orders were almost finished, and it was time to think of a new place to go. I chose Florida, Virginia, and New York. I knew I would probably get Florida or Virginia. New York required a change in rate (job), and the Navy won't do that unless there are too many people in your rate or they are about to combine rates. I popped with orders to Virginia. I was excited because I was hoping to get shore duty again. Instead, I ended up attached to a ship. A ship that was getting ready to deploy!! I was not happy about that at all. I talked to my chain of command, but there was nothing that could be done unless I wanted to get out. I didn't want to end my career so early. So, I went and did something stupid again. Yes, I'm aware I'm brainless.

I met a guy on this website called Blackplanet. He was quite handsome. He asked me out and I said yes. I should have known this was a trap. The guys and I began seeing each other. Not long after, he asked me to marry him. I said yes, not really thinking about the consequences. Also, I told him the truth, and that my ex won't be bothering us. What I didn't know was that he was having his cake and eating it too.

Puffer fish had gotten his car towed for parking in the wrong spot. He didn't have the money to pay the tow people to get his vehicle back. He had to make calls to borrow the money to get his car back. That was some of the proof to me from God that he was no good, but I thought if I 1`changed, I would be worth loving and cared about. I was so, so wrong.

I ended up not going on deployment thanks to pufferfish. I was pregnant with our first child together. On top of that, I found out pufferfish was cheating on me. I had to transfer commands due to my pregnancy. When I did the urine test, the Coreman (Navy doctor who can treat simple things) called me back within two hours of me taking it. I had an STD. Yes!!! My husband had ever so politely burned me while I was carrying his child. The way it broke me yet again. I thought moving was the answer to everything. Instead, I was being thrown away all over again.

I confronted my husband as soon as I got off the phone. This man looked me right in the face and lied to me. Then the audacity he had to tell me that I probably got the STD from a toilet seat. Sir!! I had an A in health class. We don't play these games. I knew he was hiding something, I just didn't know what. His ex-girlfriend had already messaged me a few times in the past, saying she had been in my car and our apartment before we lost it. I believed her just based on the things she could describe. Yet, I gave him another chance because the birther said my kids needed their father.

I wish I had never listened. Things ended tragically with that pregnancy. He was born prematurely because of complications from the STD. Even though I received antibiotics, the effects had already occurred. Apparently, I had the STD with no symptoms, so it did a number on me. My son paid a price for what his father had chosen to do. During my son's stay in the NICU at the hospital, my birther, her sisters, and her birther decided to come to Virginia to see my cousin and me. All of them went to visit my son one time. They saw my baby one time during their entire visit. What hurt me was that my cousin lived in the next city over. She knew what I was going through as far as dealing with a premature baby because her son had been a preemie at the exact same hospital. Her husband had been in the Navy. So, I thought it could be relational. I guess not, however. Maybe they'll just say that I didn't open my mouth enough, letting them know I was struggling and needed a lifeline.

    A few weeks later, we had to decide to let my son go. He was on a ventilator, and there was no possible way he could breathe on his own. I was so broken. I didn't want to live anymore. Pufferfish was in his own world with his own girl. My way of dealing with that was I became her friend. When she found out he was married and had been lying to her about things, she blocked him and hung out with me for some time before moving on with her life. I should have moved on with mine, too, but fear kept me bound.

I gave up on life when I lost my son. I honestly didn't want to live anymore. Things were in shambles. Between the cheating of pufferfish, issues at work, the birther and her lack of empathy and sympathy, and feeling like no one cared but a few people, I felt like I wouldn't be missed. I attempted suicide twice during this time. My pain was deep, and I didn't know how to dig it out. I just knew it needed to go before it consumed my world in a way that would leave me scarred permanently.

Digging The Knife Deeper

Time passed, and things got no better in the marriage. By the time my fourth son was born, we had moved several times. I was out of the Navy and attending school for my degree in Information Technology. I have decided to start getting therapy because I realized that I needed to fix some things in my life. I knew I couldn't do it by myself. The attachment to pufferfish had to be the beginning of the process.

At this point, the dynamics between me and my birther were different, also. She would call multiple times a day. Most of the time, she didn't want anything. There were times when I had to tell her not to call me so I could have some peace. It would be irritating. It got disrespectful a lot of the time, especially when you're trying to do schoolwork, be a wife, and take care of kids.

The dynamic between my dad and me wasn't bad, but it wasn't the greatest either. Remember the guard in jail to whom I was talking? She was Mom's sister. So, everything I said went back to her. That was not a good thing. Knowing that the things I said weren't good drove an even bigger wedge between us. I destroyed the bridge before it could even be built. I didn't know how to fix it. Things were crumbling around me.

Therapy led to medication to help stabilize my mood. Remember the blackouts from earlier in the book? At first, I was diagnosed with dissociative identity disorder. When the blackouts happened, I didn't exist during those times. Vanessa did. She played no games with anyone. When I released my first ex, they toned down to an extent. With the death of my son and dealing with pufferfish, the episodes weren't blackouts as much as they exhibited more symptoms of depressive and anxiety moods. I had a nice little list of medications, but nothing too strong that it would hurt my last baby.

I had decided with my fourth son that I was not going to get pregnant anymore. I was done with it. I saw the treatment that came from pufferfish during the pregnancies, and I saw how the lies that I had fallen for. He promised he would be one way, and gave me something else at the end of the day. When I had asked him to get a vasectomy, he said he didn't want to stop being able to have kids. So, I let him keep his freedom. I decided what I was going to do on my end. I wasn't going to blackmail him into anything. I think at that point, I knew that was a timer on the marriage; I just didn't know when the clock was going to run out.

The pregnancy went well, but once again, housing didn't, and we had to move again. We moved from North Carolina back to Virginia. The family was in a homeless shelter, which felt strange to me considering Pufferfish was able to work. Yet, there we were starting over from scratch. That was another thing I was tired of doing, too. I was done with struggling. It felt like every time I turned around, we were struggling again to make ends meet. I wanted us on our feet and staying there.

The feeling he was cheating again showed up, and I was waiting for the mess to hit the fan. We moved out of the shelter and into transitional housing. The birther would send money every once in a while to help with little things like diapers and things like that. I still tried to create boundaries with her, but I wasn't very good at it.

My health was starting to decline at the same time. I slipped the L5-S1 disc in my back. My body was hurting. Migraines were getting bad. It was like something was destroying my body, and I didn't know what it was. The number of pills I was taking had also increased, and I didn't like that either. Something had to give with that.

I want to bring up something very interesting. During this time, other "family" members have my phone number. I kept a Georgia number so there would be little to no charge for calling me. I talked to my dad often. The birther called me all the time. Mom and I weren't on the best of terms, so I knew my limits. Others, however, seemed not to be able to call and give a simple hi. Anything with them happen, I made an effort. For me, there were crickets. To be surrounded by so many people yet still feel alone hurts.

Eventually, we moved out of transitional housing and into our own apartment. I ended up having to have surgery on my back to fix the disc because it was too painful to keep ignoring. My dad and mom came to visit right before I had surgery, which was amazing. Mom's birthday was in September, and my oldest son, youngest son, and dad's birthday are all in October, so we had a birthday party for everyone, too. It was nice, and I got to introduce them to some of my

Virginia/Cali sisters. Oh yeah, almost all of my Cali sisters came to Virginia, which was so helpful when my son passed because they were my safe haven when "family" wasn't. Pufferfish made a point to stay at work and in the room. He would not interact with my parents any more than he had to. It made me wonder how he really felt about them.

    I had to go through physical therapy to recover from my surgery. It was not an easy road. My back was very uncomfortable, but I knew there was a storm coming in my life. I just didn't know it was, but I was going to be ready. The storm came a few weeks later. Pufferfish came home with a cut on his finger and leakage down below. He claims one of the girls at his job told him she had an STD, and she may have contaminated the toilet. Once again, he tried to play me for stupid. I ran to my doctor's office the next day. I found out I had bacterial vaginosis. I wanted to harm that man that day.

    I tried opening up to the birther about what was happening, but it was like she was closed off. I kept trying to tell her what I was feeling, and it was like no matter what, it was my fault. I was always making bad decisions, and I just needed to suck it up for the kids. According to her, I needed to stop complaining and just pray about it. Yet, guess who was calling daily, asking what was going on with me?

There were a few other issues of contention with me. Every time I talked to my birther about a medical issue, she magically had the same one. I would want to do something, and she wanted to do the same thing. Like, why are you trying to live my life? You had yours. I certainly don't want to do anything you did, and I don't need you acting like me. It was becoming a sore spot for me. Oddly, though, pufferfish was standing up for her. I didn't think about it then, but looking back, it was odd because he didn't really care for any of the people in my life but her.

I was still in therapy for my mental health. I felt like I was losing my mind with everything happening. One good thing that happened, though, was that my diagnosis changed to C-PTSD (Chronic PTSD) with bipolar disorder. This made way so that the veterans' benefits I had been fighting for since losing my son could be approved. Receiving that changed something for me. I believe it was a tendril inside being released. Like I knew that if I were ever to step away from that man, it would be ok because there was permanent money there that would take care of me and my children. Somehow, I had a little less fear.

Worst Time In My Life

Once again, we were moving. Back to North Carolina we went. I had made up my mind with this move that I was going to make the effort to spend more time with the Georgia family. I just felt this urgency to see them more. I was glad I did. Not long after the move, we found out my aunt had ALS. My heart was broken. My aunt was the closest person to a mom that I had, next to my stepmom. I loved her so much. My sons loved her too, especially my oldest. She had a hand in raising him, too, while I was gone. My oldest had already experience death. Now he was going to have to deal with it again. My middle and youngest were going to deal with it for the first time, and I was going to lose another important person in my life.

    I treasured each day I got to hear from my aunt. At the same time, my own health wasn't doing the best. I was making many trips to the hospital—kidney stones, back pain, migraines, body aches, insomnia, vertigo, and more. Many times, I felt like my body didn't even belong to me. On top of that, I was being treated at the VA (Veteran Affairs) offices, and it felt like I was being ignored more than anything. The more I complained about the forms of treatments, or the lack thereof in some areas, the more I seemed to have problems with getting the answers I was trying to find. Pufferfish claimed he was helping and talking to the doctors, but somehow I think he was doing the opposite, based on the reactions I received. I honestly believe he told them I was crazy and that something was wrong with me mentally. Especially based on the birther. His goal was not to help me.

During all of this, I felt the need to go back to writing. I decided to go to books instead of poetry. I talked to my then-therapist about the idea, and she felt it was a good idea. Granted, I later fired her, but that was for her ignoring me regarding something medical. I wrote my first book, "Bondage", which later became "I'm Still Standing Here." I wanted to really express what I felt dealing with having a parent who didn't act like a parent, and being in an abusive relationship with a narcissist. I wondered about just writing the book and leaving it at that, or publishing it. With encouragement from my sisters, my dad, and mom, and some others, I decided to publish the book, along with two cookbooks I had created, too. The thing about that was pufferfish was not happy about me publishing the book.

Even though I had let him know that I wanted to publish the book, and he never said not to publish it, he was mad that I published it. He was mad that I was telling people about my first marriage, like there was shame that I had been married before. I was wondering if there was shame I had been married before, or was there anger because of the choices I made with my first that I didn't make with him? I was going to get the answers to that question, and realize that I wish that I had stayed oblivious.

The book did more than just allow me to open up about my wounds and scars. It opened me to a community of women (and some men) who had been through the same. At the same time, it made my birther close down like Ft. Knox. She did not like me bringing up the past. She and her birther were big on I couldn't bring up things from before. Yet they could always remind me of everything that happened in my past. I needed the door opened. I needed to face it, deal with it, heal from on, and be able to move on. It felt like moving on was supposed to be their decision, not mine, or they move on, and it didn't matter if I moved on or not. Just suck it up and keep it pushing because that's just what you do. That's generational trauma, and I wasn't going to continue it, and I wasn't going to pass it to my children. How was I supposed to stop it when it was weighing me down on every side?

I decided to revamp myself again this process and be more feminine by playing with makeup again. I would do little videos and take pictures. I would play with my hair, doing different styles and colors with yarn. Pufferfish and my birther had issues with that. Both of them would find an issue with something. One would find a problem with the color. The other would say I was doing too much. There was a problem with my clothes. I was at the point where they should have been together or something. Maybe they were teaming up on purpose to destroy me because I was over it. I was tired. I was doing nothing right.

On top of that, we wanted to move again. The birther wanted me to help her copy me again, too. Why? Just why? I was at the point where I was ready to escape and be by myself for a while. I didn't want to be around anyone, especially not the two of them. In the process, my aunt passed. Another chamber of my heart was gone. We moved to a city called Fayetteville, NC. I thought things would look up being there. I didn't know that this would be my city of transition.

This was the place where we finally moved into a house. That was a dream I always had. I wanted to move into a house. The goal was always to own a home at some point. I wanted the kids to have stability. I was done with constantly moving. The kids were too. Pufferfish didn't seem to care either way. The kids and I realized that as we wanted something more permanent, there were things that were starting to drift apart. Somehow, God was separating things.

The first couple of years were relatively uneventful. When the pandemic came around, it was crazy. It came in right before my oldest was getting ready to graduate from high school. He was glad for the pandemic because he was tired of school, not the academics as much as dealing with people. He'd spent most of his academic life bullied and fighting. His grades didn't suffer despite dealing with these people who thought that being smart was dumb. I understood how he felt, considering I had been through the same. It hammered down my resolve to keep my middle and youngest from going through the same. I saw signs of it starting to happen already before the pandemic began. The pandemic was the answer from God that I needed to take my kids out of school and never send them back.

Now, pufferfish was not in agreement, but I overrode him. I had tried to do the same for my oldest when he was in seventh grade, but I caved and sent him back the next year, listening to pufferfish. I would not fail my kids that way ever again. It was insane to me that he would even think that way, considering he had suffered bullying himself. I guess being a hoe now boosted his ego into thinking that it didn't matter anymore. I was going to do what he refused to do.

I had started therapy again through Veterans Affairs. I was working on getting betting medical treatment. I got an amazing doctor and therapist at the same time. When I tell you both were everything I needed. I began to see that it was becoming time to start facing some of my demons and letting some people go in my life. I had left too many doors open.

Staying in the marriage was literally killing me. I needed to decide what to do about things before I didn't get the chance to see my children grow up.

In March 2021, I was sitting in the waiting area outside the lab in the VA office. My name was called, and I stood up to walk to the door. I was slightly dizzy, but I thought I could power through it like I normally did. My heart started pounding, and everything turned black. I woke up on the floor. One of the male nurses had caught me. I was rushed to the hospital to be checked over to make sure I didn't have a heart attack because my blood pressure was so high. Fear gripped me that something was going to go wrong.

Three months later, my dad got sick. His kidneys were going bad. He had to start dialysis. My world was starting to fall apart all over again, and I didn't know what to do about it. I was scared I was going to lose him. I am a daddy's girl, and I can't imagine what my world would look like without my dad in it. My heart is already broken for so many of my sisters because they have lost their dad. I don't want to lose mine.

The next year comes in, and I go to visit Georgia. We do a family trip to Disney. It wasn't the best trip. Where I should have been spending time trying to interact, I was standoffish. I withheld myself. I didn't want to open myself up. Yes, I know I punked out. I'm a scaredy cat. I've apologized to Mama for things I said before, yet I've never really done more than that.

We left, then came back to Georgia later that same year. I had made up my mind about leaving my marriage. Two factors helped me come to my conclusion. The first was my not getting over being accused of being at fault for the death of our son, even though he was the one who was dead. The second was that I was feeling toward him like I did toward my birther. Except there were no blackouts. There was just a want to kill him. I'm not violent, so that was not normal. I refuse to go to prison over someone like that.

When I told my birther my decision, she told me that I may as well stay with him. She had the audacity to say I would never find anyone like him, and he was the best thing that would ever happen to me. I couldn't believe she would say that to me after knowing the fourteen years of hell I went through with him, as if she didn't look at her grandson inside the incubator on a ventilator. I sent her pictures every single day up until the day he died. This woman acted like I didn't cry my soul out on the phone for weeks after his death when she would call me. I was at a loss. I couldn't even anymore.

I began to talk to her less and less through the year of separation. I talked to him less, too. Things were just too messy. I had started healing in a way I needed. I received the medical records from my second son. That did so much for me. I had spent years trying to get those records so I could see his treatments and if the military had done an autopsy. They had, and it solidified what I knew. My son's death was only my fault in that I trusted the wrong man to be his father.

I began school, working on my bachelor's in psychology with a concentration in Mental Health Counseling. I wrote my book on my son's life and death, my second marriage and divorce, my three suicide attempts, and I even wrote a Christian romance. I graduated, bought a house, and moved to another state. I rededicated my life to Christ, and burned to ash for the last time for people.

No More Trying

Now we are here. I named this chapter this because that's where I'm at now. I'm sure a lot of you are at this point in your life. You're done trying to build a relationship with the woman who birthed you. You're over being manipulated by her. Pushed around by her. She keeps talking down to you. You're tired of her treating you like dirt.

I reached my breaking point last summer. I ended up in the hospital in severe pain. It was so severe that the local emergency room couldn't figure out what was causing it and was limited in controlling it. So, they transferred me to their primary hospital for more testing and pain control. It was to the point where I had to put on morphine. I had let my church family know what was going on so they could check in with my kids. My oldest had everything under control, yet I have church parents, and I know they will want to make sure everything is good, too. I had my oldest let my dad know what was going on, then I made a post on Facebook. I wanted to see how long it would take to receive a phone call.

Within minutes, my text messages, Messenger, and Instagram, everything were all lighting up. Yet, there was no phone call from my birther. The meds had me sleeping off and on. My pastor called to check on me. My moms called to check on me. When I say moms, I mean my spiritual moms, the moms God gave me on the church side, and my friends' moms who have adopted me. My brother, who was overseas, checked in—nothing from her. Forty-eight hours later, she calls. She had just heard that I was in the hospital. That was the final chance.

    I went home in August of last year for my graduation party. It was the last time she saw my children and my face. I am honest with my children about everything. We have real conversations. They have seen what has happened. I have been honest with them about how my birther treated me, and how I treated Mama. We have had candid conversations and ways to deal with both situations. Hands are washed of the birther. She is in God's hands. We pray that all is well with her. We have done a Romans 12:18. It is no longer possible with her. We have done it with a majority of the water on that side. It has not worked. So, like the Bible says, we shake the dust off our feet, and we go on. I'm the kind of person who, if you hate me, just say so. I will that much less effort. I have no problem loving you from a distance.

I promise it's ok to have that heart. Love them from a distance. Stop forcing yourself on a person who will never accept you. My heart breaks every time I see another daughter who is broken by the woman who was supposed to build her. Then she's angry at her for the result. She lashes at her for not fighting back, yet she's why she can't fight back. Not realizing that the same daughter she broke is the same one she's going to need later.

The other day, I saw that it was saying psychologists are finding that mother-daughter relationships have an effect on how women's friendships with other women. I shook my head at how late they are to the game. I figured that out for myself. Mine made me not trust other women for a long time. So many of us carry this hurt, and we don't know how to tell anyone how bad it's been. I saw where Tina Turner said her mother was so proud of her for being famous, but she still never liked her. Her mother liked her money, but never liked her. That has to be one of the most painful things to think about when you look at the person who birthed you when they come around you.

    My hope and prayer is that this book gives someone the courage to step out and walk away. You deserve to be loved. If the people who are supposed to be "family" can throw you away, it's ok to stay away. I promise you, God will replace them with a family that will never throw you away and will always be there for you. God will never throw you away. He created you. The only one who can separate you from Him is you. Nothing can separate us from the love of God, only us. I love you, and God loves you.